RIGHTSTART™ MATHEMATICS

by Joan A. Cotter, Ph.D.
with Tracy Mittleider, MSEd

LEVEL B WORKSHEETS
Second Edition

A *Activities for Learning, Inc.*

A special thank you to Kathleen Cotter Clayton for all her work on the preparation of this manual.

Copyright © 2013, 2024 by Activities for Learning, Inc.

All rights reserved. No part of this publication may be reproduced, stored in a retrieval system, or transmitted, in any form or by any means, electronic, mechanical, photocopying, recording, or otherwise, without written permission of Activities for Learning, Inc.

The publisher hereby grants permission to reproduce the worksheets for a single child's use only.

Printed in the United States of America

www.RightStartMath.com

For more information: info@RightStartMath.com
Supplies may be ordered from: www.RightStartMath.com

Activities for Learning, Inc.
321 Hill Street
Hazelton, ND 58544-0468
United States of America
888-775-6284 or 701-782-2000
701-782-2007 fax

ISBN 978-1-931980-63-0

May 2024

GAME LOG

Math games are an important part of the RightStart™ Mathematics program. Instead of flash-cards or timed tests, games supply the necessary repetition for understanding and mastery in an enjoyable setting, providing a superior educational atmosphere. The lessons indicate which games to play. Additional games can be found in the *Math Card Games* book.

This Game Log provides a record of the games played and when they were played.

Date	Game Played	Players

Games help you understand, apply, and enjoy mathematics.

GAME LOG CONTINUED

Date	Game Played	Players

Games help you understand, apply, and enjoy mathematics.

© Activities for Learning, Inc. 2013, 2024

GAME LOG CONTINUED

Date	Game Played	Players

Games help you understand, apply, and enjoy mathematics.

© Activities for Learning, Inc. 2013, 2024

GAME LOG CONTINUED

Date	Game Played	Players

Games help you understand, apply, and enjoy mathematics.

© Activities for Learning, Inc. 2013, 2024

Worksheet 1, Subitizing Quantities 1 to 10

Name: _____

Date: _____

Match the quantities.

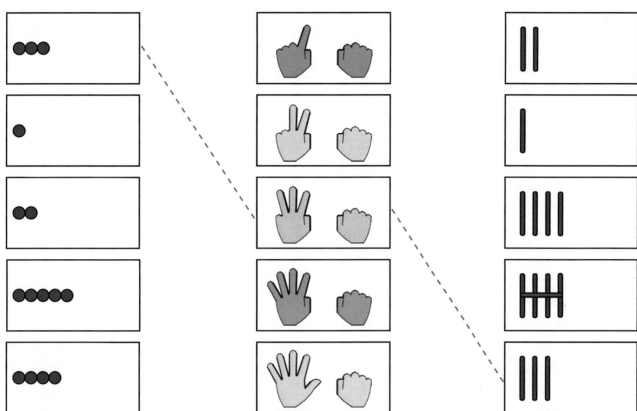

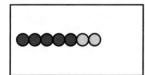 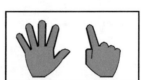 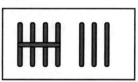

 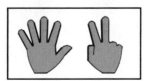 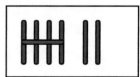

 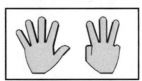 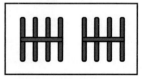

 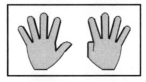 

 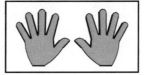 

Worksheet 2, Partitioning with Part-Whole Circle Sets

Name: _____

Date: _____

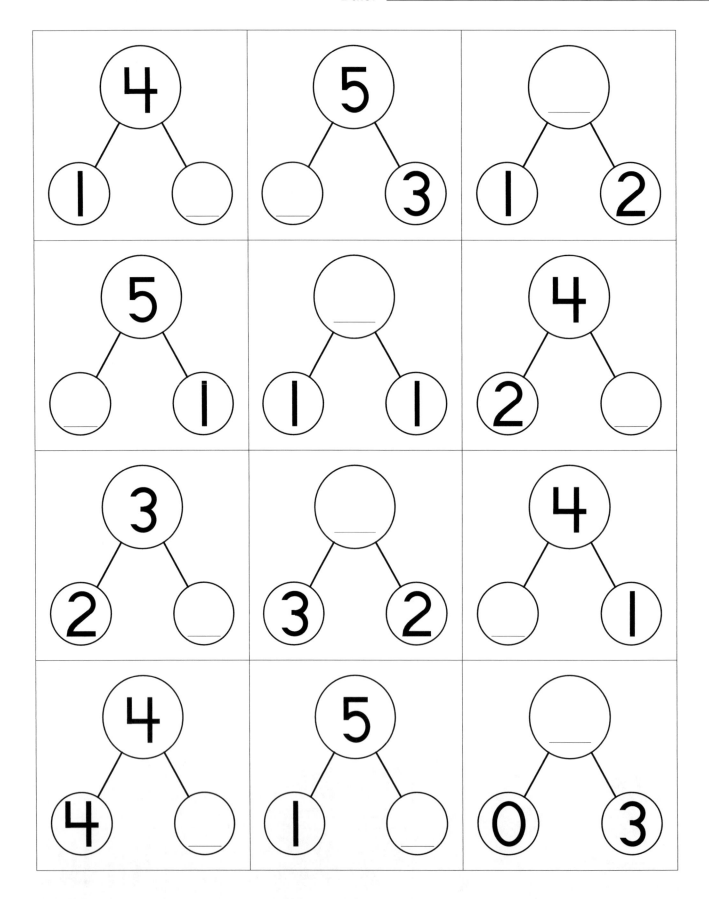

Worksheet 2, Partitioning with Part-Whole Circle Sets

Worksheet 3, Writing Addition Equations

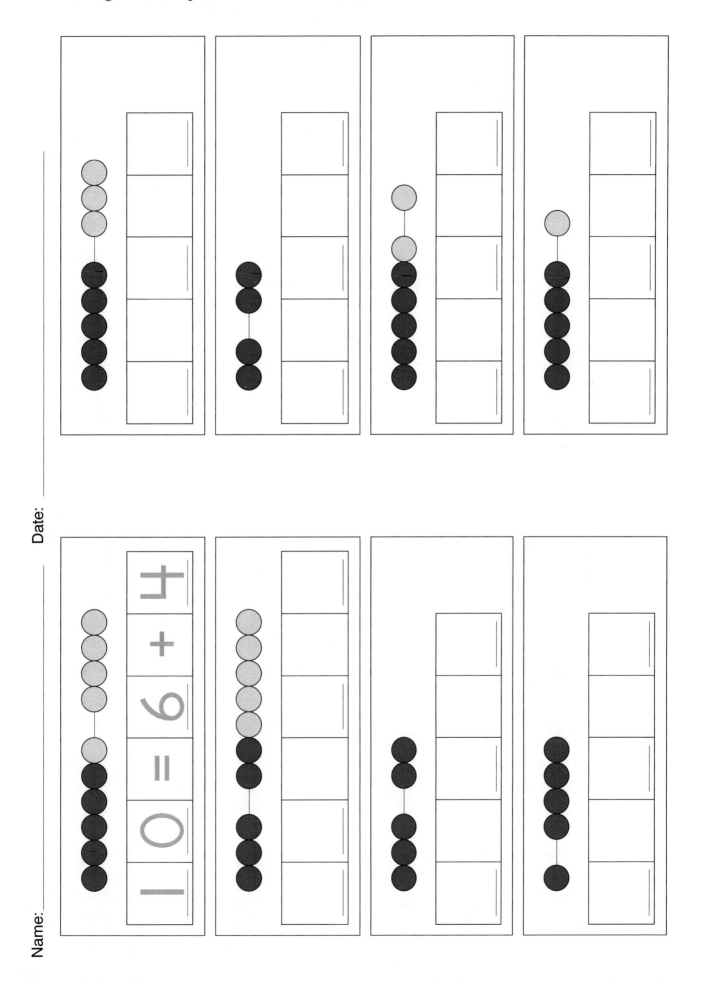

Worksheet 4, Tens and Ones

Name: _____

Date: _____

6	0	+	7	=		
3	0	+	3	=		
5	0	+	6	=		
1	0	+	2	=		
9	0	+	4	=		

7	8	=	7	0	+
2	1	=	2	0	+
6	3	=	6	0	+
8	9	=			+
4	5	=			+

RightStart™ Mathematics second edition, B

© Activities for Learning, Inc. 2013, 2024

Worksheet 5, Evens and Odds

					odd	even
					odd	even
					odd	even
					odd	even
					odd	even

RightStart™ Mathematics second edition, B

Worksheet 6, The Commutative Property

Name: _____

Date: _____

$7 + 2 =$
$2 + 7 =$

$3 + 5 =$
$5 + 3 =$

$7 + 1 =$
$1 + 7 =$

$3 + 7 =$
$7 + 3 =$

$4 + 5 =$
$5 + 4 =$

$6 + 3 =$
$3 + 6 =$

$4 + 3 =$
$3 + 4 =$

$8 + 1 =$
$1 + 8 =$

RightStart™ Mathematics second edition, B

© Activities for Learning, Inc. 2013, 2024

Worksheet 7, Solving "Add To" Problems

Name: _____

Date: _____

Use the part-whole circle sets to solve the problems. Then write the complete equation and underline the answer.

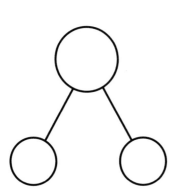

Sam has 9 crayons. Then Sam gets 2 more crayons from a box. How many crayons does Sam have now?

_____

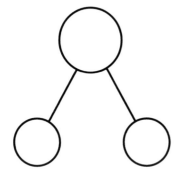

Jacob saw 2 butterflies on a flower. Some more butterflies landed on the flower. Now he sees 8 butterflies. How many butterflies landed on the flower?

_____

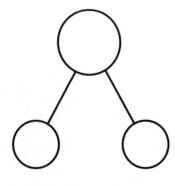

Emily got 4 goldfish for her birthday. Now she has 8 goldfish. How many goldfish did she have before her birthday?

_____

Jack picked 8 apples. Jill picked the same amount. How many apples did they pick together?

_____

_____

Worksheet 8, Adding Ten to a Number

Name: _____

Date: _____

49 + 10 = _____

23 + 10 = _____

51 + 10 = _____

18 + 10 = _____

65 + 10 = _____

4 + 10 = _____

76 + 10 = _____

82 + 10 = _____

37 + 10 = _____

RightStart™ Mathematics second edition, B   © Activities for Learning, Inc. 2013, 2024

Worksheet 9, Adding Ones and Adding Tens

Name: _____

Date: _____

5 + 2 =
50 + 20 =

4 + 4 =
40 + 40 =

7 + 2 =
70 + 20 =

2 + 6 =
20 + 60 =

4 + 2 =
40 + 20 =

8 + 1 =
80 + 10 =

3 + 4 =
30 + 40 =

4 + 5 =
40 + 50 =

Worksheet 10, Two-Fives Strategy

Name: _____

Date: _____

$6 + 8 =$ _____	$9 + 5 =$ _____
$9 + 7 =$ _____	$6 + 7 =$ _____
$6 + 9 =$ _____	$8 + 5 =$ _____
$6 + 5 =$ _____	$7 + 9 =$ _____
$9 + 6 =$ _____	$5 + 6 =$ _____
$7 + 5 =$ _____	$5 + 9 =$ _____
$9 + 8 =$ _____	$7 + 6 =$ _____
$8 + 9 =$ _____	$7 + 8 =$ _____
$6 + 6 =$ _____	$8 + 6 =$ _____
$8 + 7 =$ _____	$5 + 7 =$ _____
$7 + 7 =$ _____	$8 + 8 =$ _____
	$5 + 8 =$ _____

RightStart™ Mathematics second edition, B

© Activities for Learning, Inc. 2013, 2024

Worksheet 11, Solving "Combine" Problems

Name: _____

Date: _____

Use the part-whole circle sets to solve the problems, then write the complete equation and underline the answer.

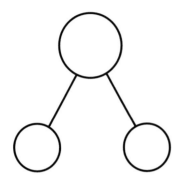

Levi has 6 red apples and 9 green apples to sell. How many apples does Levi have to sell?

_____

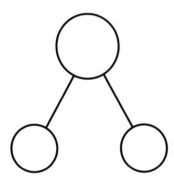

There are 15 children playing tag. In the group, 7 children are girls. How many of the children are boys?

_____

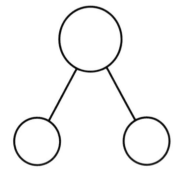

Lydia is waiting for her birthday. There are 5 days in May and 10 days in June until her birthday. How many days must Lydia wait?

_____

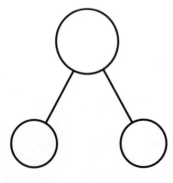

There are 12 months in a year. Two months start with the letter A. How many months do not start with A?

_____

_____

Worksheet 12, Review
Page1

Name: _____

Date: _____

1–4. Write what comes next in the following patterns.

6, 7, 8, _____

28, 29, 30, _____

98, 99, 100, _____

107, 108, 109, _____

5–7. What is 70 + 1? _____

Now add 1 again. What is the answer? _____

Continue adding 1 till all the blanks are filled.

_____ _____ _____ _____ _____ _____ _____ _____

8. Build the even stairs on the abacus. Write the even numbers in the blanks.

_____ _____ _____ _____ _____

9. Build the odd stairs on the abacus. Write the odd numbers in the blanks.

_____ _____ _____ _____ _____

10–22. Complete the following addition problems.

2+4= ___	6+6= ___
2+7= ___	4+3= ___
4+4= ___	3+4= ___
42+10= ___	

RightStart™ Mathematics second edition, B

© Activities for Learning, Inc. 2013, 2024

Worksheet 12, Review
Page 2

Name: _____

Date: _____

8 + 1 = ___	9 + 7 = ___
80 + 10 = ___	35 + 5 = ___
6 + 8 = ___	70 + 15 = ___

23–25. Use the part-whole circle sets to solve the problems. Then write the complete equation.

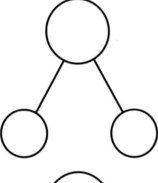

Emma has 4 books on the desk. Then Emma gets 5 more books from a box. How many books does Emma have on the desk now?

_____

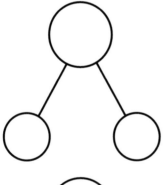

There are 3 boys and 6 girls at the swimming pool. How many kids are at the swimming pool?

_____

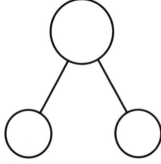

Six hundred trees are to be planted in a park. Three hundred trees have already been planted. How many more trees must still be planted?

_____

26. Circle all the rectangles.

Worksheet 13, Assessment 1
Page 1

Name: _____

Date: _____

1–3. Write what comes next in the following patterns.

3, 4, 5, _____

48, 49, 50, _____

107, 108, 109, _____

4–6. What is 50 + 1? _____

Now add 1 again. What is the answer? _____

Continue adding 1 till all the blanks are filled.

_____ _____ _____ _____ _____ _____ _____ _____

7. Build the even stairs on the abacus. Write the even numbers in the blanks starting with 6.

_____ _____ _____ _____ _____

8. Build the odd stairs on the abacus. Write the odd numbers in the blanks starting with 3.

_____ _____ _____ _____ _____

9–21. Complete the following addition problems.

2+8 = ___	8+8 = ___
2+5 = ___	5+3 = ___
5+5 = ___	3+5 = ___
74+10 = ___	

Worksheet 13, Assessment 1
Page 2

Name: _____
Date: _____

6 + 1 = ___	8 + 5 = ___
60 + 10 = ___	65 + 5 = ___
6 + 9 = ___	80 + 15 = ___

22–27. Use the part-whole circle sets to solve the problems. Then write the complete equation.

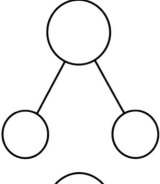

Danny has 6 pillows on the bed. Then Danny gets 5 more pillows from the closet. How many pillows does Danny have on the bed now?

_____

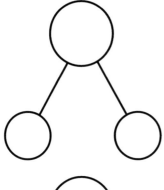

There are 4 boys and 5 girls at the park. How many kids are at the park?

_____

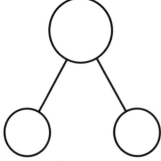

Five hundred trees are to be planted in a park. Four hundred trees have already been planted. How many more trees must still be planted?

_____

25–27. Name the shapes below.

Worksheet 14, Designs with Diagonals

Name: _____

Date: _____

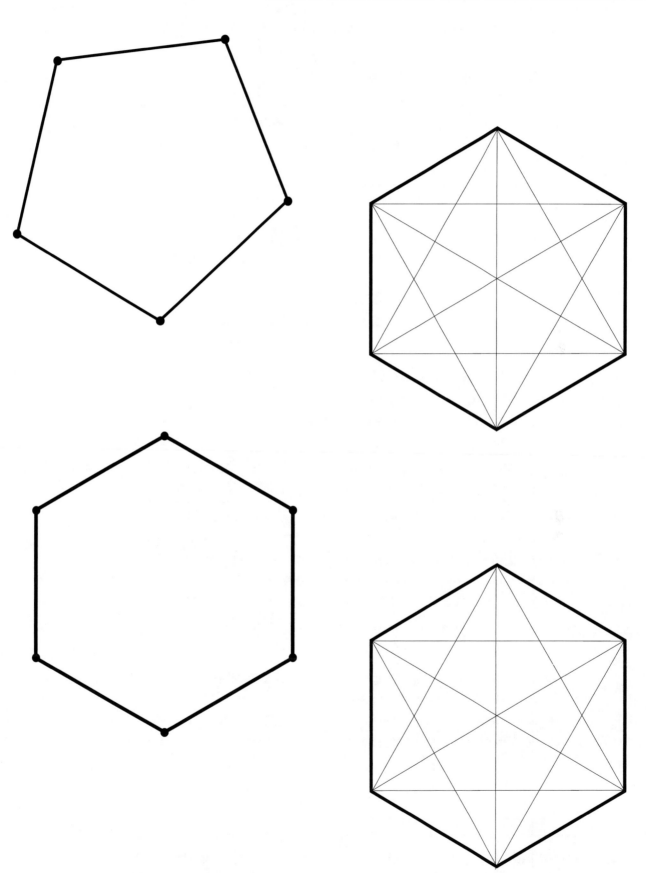

Worksheet 15, The Greater Than Symbol

Name: _____

Date: _____

$$6 \bigcirc 4$$

$$9 \bigcirc 7$$

$$17 \bigcirc 17$$

$$31 \bigcirc 13$$

$$8+3 \bigcirc 4+6$$

$$21+10 \bigcirc 31$$

$$60+5 \bigcirc 50+6$$

$$7+8 \bigcirc 8+7$$

$$1+90 \bigcirc 19$$

$$200 \bigcirc 50+50$$

$$110 \bigcirc 100+1$$

Worksheet 16, Adding 9 to a Number

Name: _____

Date: _____

	$9 + 9 =$ _____
$9 + 3 =$ _____	$9 + 4 =$ _____
$9 + 7 =$ _____	$9 + 2 =$ _____
$3 + 9 =$ _____	$5 + 9 =$ _____
$9 + 8 =$ _____	$9 + 5 =$ _____
$6 + 9 =$ _____	$7 + 9 =$ _____
$4 + 9 =$ _____	$8 + 9 =$ _____

$79 + 5 =$ _____	$19 + 8 =$ _____
$59 + 4 =$ _____	$29 + 6 =$ _____
$89 + 2 =$ _____	$15 + 9 =$ _____
$69 + 9 =$ _____	$49 + 1 =$ _____
$33 + 9 =$ _____	$57 + 9 =$ _____

RightStart™ Mathematics second edition, B   © Activities for Learning, Inc. 2013, 2024

Worksheet 17, Adding 8 to a Number

Name: _____

Date: _____

	$3 + 8 =$ _____
$8 + 6 =$ _____	$4 + 8 =$ _____
$8 + 8 =$ _____	$9 + 8 =$ _____
$8 + 9 =$ _____	$8 + 5 =$ _____
$5 + 8 =$ _____	$7 + 8 =$ _____
$2 + 8 =$ _____	$6 + 8 =$ _____
$8 + 4 =$ _____	$8 + 3 =$ _____

$18 + 8 =$ _____	$78 + 8 =$ _____
$68 + 7 =$ _____	$18 + 2 =$ _____
$58 + 6 =$ _____	$28 + 5 =$ _____
$38 + 4 =$ _____	$88 + 9 =$ _____
$28 + 3 =$ _____	$48 + 5 =$ _____

RightStart™ Mathematics second edition, B   © Activities for Learning, Inc. 2013, 2024

Worksheet 18, Two-Fives Strategy Practice

Name: _____

Date: _____

To see the pattern, mark the squares that are the same as your answers.

1	2	3	4	5	6	7	8	9	10
11	12	13	14	15	16	17	18	19	20
21	22	23	24	25	26	27	28	29	30
31	32	33	34	35	36	37	38	39	40
41	42	43	44	45	46	47	48	49	50
51	52	53	54	55	56	57	58	59	60
61	62	63	64	65	66	67	68	69	70
71	72	73	74	75	76	77	78	79	80
81	82	83	84	85	86	87	88	89	90
91	92	93	94	95	96	97	98	99	100

$56 + 6 =$ _____

$57 + 7 =$ _____

$47 + 6 =$ _____

$88 + 6 =$ _____

$76 + 7 =$ _____

$37 + 5 =$ _____

$85 + 8 =$ _____

$77 + 5 =$ _____

$66 + 7 =$ _____

$57 + 6 =$ _____

$66 + 6 =$ _____

$85 + 7 =$ _____

$45 + 7 =$ _____

$67 + 7 =$ _____

$76 + 8 =$ _____

RightStart™ Mathematics second edition, B

© Activities for Learning, Inc. 2013, 2024

Worksheet 19, Adding 8s and 9s Practice

Name: _____   Date: _____

To see the pattern, mark the squares that are the same as your answers.

1	2	3	4	5	6	7	8	9	10
11	12	13	14	15	16	17	18	19	20
21	22	23	24	25	26	27	28	29	30
31	32	33	34	35	36	37	38	39	40
41	42	43	44	45	46	47	48	49	50
51	52	53	54	55	56	57	58	59	60
61	62	63	64	65	66	67	68	69	70
71	72	73	74	75	76	77	78	79	80
81	82	83	84	85	86	87	88	89	90
91	92	93	94	95	96	97	98	99	100

$4 + 8 =$ _____

$9 + 9 =$ _____

$49 + 7 =$ _____

$18 + 5 =$ _____

$46 + 8 =$ _____

$69 + 3 =$ _____

$37 + 8 =$ _____

$78 + 3 =$ _____

$69 + 9 =$ _____

$54 + 9 =$ _____

$18 + 9 =$ _____

$28 + 8 =$ _____

$81 + 8 =$ _____

$25 + 9 =$ _____

$59 + 8 =$ _____

RightStart™ Mathematics second edition, B

© Activities for Learning, Inc. 2013, 2024

Worksheet 20, More Adding with Base-10 Cards

Name: _____

Date: _____

A.

$$\begin{array}{r} 2\ 8\ 3\ 4 \\ +\ 5\ 7\ 1\ 8 \\ \hline \end{array}$$

B.

$$\begin{array}{r} 2\ 4\ 7\ 3 \\ +\ 3\ 6\ 4\ 7 \\ \hline \end{array}$$

C.

$$\begin{array}{r} 4\ 7\ 9\ 1 \\ +\ 1\ 2\ 8\ 8 \\ \hline \end{array}$$

D.

$$\begin{array}{r} 2\ 6\ 4\ 9 \\ +\ 1\ 8\ 7\ 7 \\ \hline \end{array}$$

E.

$$\begin{array}{r} 1\ 5\ 0\ 9 \\ +\ 3\ 2\ 4\ 6 \\ \hline \end{array}$$

F.

$$\begin{array}{r} 1\ 6\ 7\ 8 \\ +\ 3\ 5\ 2\ 9 \\ \hline \end{array}$$

RightStart™ Mathematics second edition, B

© Activities for Learning, Inc. 2013, 2024

Worksheet 21, Adding Several Numbers

Name: _____

Date: _____

$3 + 2 + 1 =$ ___

$5 + 2 + 2 =$ ___

$4 + 3 + 2 =$ ___

$1 + 2 + 7 =$ ___

$2 + 3 + 6 =$ ___

$3 + 5 + 5 =$ ___

$2 + 7 + 8 =$ ___

$10 + 2 + 3 =$ ___

$6 + 5 + 6 =$ ___

$2 + 9 + 9 =$ ___

RightStart™ Mathematics second edition, B

© Activities for Learning, Inc. 2013, 2024

Worksheet 22, Solving Problems with Three Addends

Name: _____

Date: _____

James picked 3 red flowers, 6 blue flowers, and 7 yellow flowers. How many flowers did James pick?

_____

On a trail, Kaitlyn saw 4 children riding bicycles, 10 children walking, and 1 child getting a drink. How many children did Kaitlyn see?

_____

Alex has 3 chapter books, 2 nursery rhyme books, and 8 picture books. How many books does Alex have?

_____

Michael and Matthew each have 6 shoes. Matilda has 8 shoes. How many shoes do the three children have in all?

_____

RightStart™ Mathematics second edition, B   © Activities for Learning, Inc. 2013, 2024

Worksheet 23, Adding 2-Digit Numbers and Tens

Name: _____ Date: _____

To see the pattern, mark the squares that are the same as your answers.

1	2	3	4	5	6	7	8	9	10
11	12	13	14	15	16	17	18	19	20
21	22	23	24	25	26	27	28	29	30
31	32	33	34	35	36	37	38	39	40
41	42	43	44	45	46	47	48	49	50
51	52	53	54	55	56	57	58	59	60
61	62	63	64	65	66	67	68	69	70
71	72	73	74	75	76	77	78	79	80
81	82	83	84	85	86	87	88	89	90
91	92	93	94	95	96	97	98	99	100

16 + 20 = _____

34 + 50 = _____

27 + 20 = _____

15 + 20 = _____

18 + 40 = _____

35 + 60 = _____

33 + 40 = _____

27 + 60 = _____

19 + 50 = _____

33 + 20 = _____

26 + 70 = _____

14 + 30 = _____

22 + 40 = _____

46 + 50 = _____

65 + 30 = _____

28 + 50 = _____

RightStart™ Mathematics second edition, B

© Activities for Learning, Inc. 2013, 2024

Worksheet 24, Mentally Adding 2-Digit Numbers

Name: _____

Date: _____

$21 + 15 =$ _____

$15 + 17 =$ _____

$29 + 36 =$ _____

$19 + 19 =$ _____

$24 + 43 =$ _____

$37 + 26 =$ _____

$64 + 36 =$ _____

$67 + 29 =$ _____

$41 + 59 =$ _____

$27 + 67 =$ _____

$16 + 18 =$ _____

$28 + 37 =$ _____

To see the pattern, mark the squares that match as your answers. Some answers are the same.

1	2	3	4	5	6	7	8	9	10
11	12	13	14	15	16	17	18	19	20
21	22	23	24	25	26	27	28	29	30
31	32	33	34	35	36	37	38	39	40
41	42	43	44	45	46	47	48	49	50
51	52	53	54	55	56	57	58	59	60
61	62	63	64	65	66	67	68	69	70
71	72	73	74	75	76	77	78	79	80
81	82	83	84	85	86	87	88	89	90
91	92	93	94	95	96	97	98	99	100

$53 + 45 =$ _____

$36 + 56 =$ _____

$12 + 57 =$ _____

$15 + 25 =$ _____

Worksheet 25, Adding 1, 10, and 100

Name: _____   Date: _____

Add 1 to each number.

4	___
67	___
99	___
200	___
238	___
493	___
790	___
906	___
1010	___
3025	___

Add 10 to each number.

4	___
67	___
99	___
200	___
238	___
493	___
790	___
906	___
1010	___
3025	___

Add 100 to each number.

4	___
67	___
99	___
200	___
238	___
493	___
790	___
906	___
1010	___
3025	___

RightStart™ Mathematics second edition, B

© Activities for Learning, Inc. 2013, 2024

Worksheet 26, Adding 4-Digit Numbers

Name: _____

Date: _____

```
    1 4 3 8            2 9 4 8
 +  6 3 8 1         +  5 6 4 5
 _____        _____


    3 4 5 4            4 8 2 1
 +  5 4 3 6         +  1 4 8 1
 _____        _____


    5 0 9 5            6 4 7 6
 +  3 5 6 4         +  2 5 9 2
 _____        _____


    7 7 4 4            8 1 6 3
 +  1 9 6 7         +    3 3 7
 _____        _____
```

RightStart™ Mathematics second edition, B   © Activities for Learning, Inc. 2013, 2024

Worksheet 27, Continuing the Pattern

Name: _____

Date: _____

Find the pattern. Write the numbers that come next.

7	8	9	___	___
10	12	14	___	___
30	40	50	___	___
60	65	70	___	___
24	26	28	___	___
15	20	25	___	___
86	87	88	___	___
77	78	79	___	___
76	78	80	___	___
60	70	80	___	___
35	40	45	___	___
14	16	18	___	___

RightStart™ Mathematics second edition, B

© Activities for Learning, Inc. 2013, 2024

Worksheet 28, Review
Page1

Name: _____

Date: _____

1. Circle the ABC pattern.

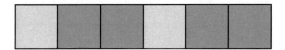 

2. Circle the increasing pattern.

3–4. Draw a rectangle and put a dot at a vertex. Then draw a diagonal line from that vertex.

5–7. Insert the > or = symbol to make the equations correct.

| 6 ◯ 4 | 7+8 ◯ 8+7 | 200 ◯ 50+50 |

8–13. Complete the following problems using the strategies learned in previous lessons.

79 + 5 = _____   59 + 4 = _____

38 + 4 = _____   68 + 7 = _____

47 + 6 = _____   88 + 6 = _____

14. How many 1s in 10? _____

15. How many 10s in 100? _____

16. How many 100s in 1000? _____

Worksheet 28, Review
Page2

Name: _____

Date: _____

17–18. Fill in the part-whole circle sets with correct numbers.

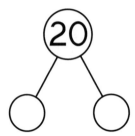 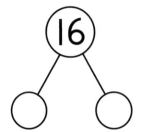

19. 3 + 5 + 5 = _____

20. 2 + 7 + 8 = _____

21. 10 + 2 + 3 = _____

22. 18 + 40 = _____

23. 35 + 60 = _____

24. How many days are in a year? _____

25. How many days are in a leap year? _____

26–29. Add with your abacus and write the answers.

```
  1438          2948
 +6381         +5645
```

```
  3454          4821
 +5436         +1481
```

Worksheet 29, Assessment 2
Page 1

Name: _____

Date: _____

1. Circle the ABC pattern.

2. Circle the increasing pattern.

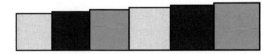 

3–4. Draw a square and put a dot at a vertex. Then draw a diagonal line from that vertex.

5–7. Insert the > or = symbols to make the equations correct.

 6+8 ○ 8+6   300 ○ 60+60   7 ○ 5

8–13. Complete the following problems using the strategies learned in previous lessons.

89 + 5 = _____   49 + 4 = _____

48 + 4 = _____   78 + 7 = _____

37 + 6 = _____   78 + 6 = _____

14. How many 1s in 10? _____

15. How many 10s in 100? _____

16. How many 100s in 1000? _____

Worksheet 29, Assessment 2
Page2

Name: _____

Date: _____

17–18. Fill in the part-whole circle sets with correct numbers.

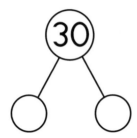 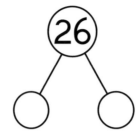

19. 5 + 5 + 5 = _____

20. 3 + 6 + 9 = _____

21. 11 + 1 + 4 = _____

22. 28 + 40 = _____

23. 35 + 50 = _____

24. How many days are in a week? _____

25. How many days are in a year? _____

26. How many days are in a leap year? _____

27–29. Add with your abacus and write the answers.

$$\begin{array}{r}1488\\+3631\\\hline\end{array}\qquad\begin{array}{r}4298\\+4565\\\hline\end{array}$$

$$\begin{array}{r}4534\\+3654\\\hline\end{array}\qquad\begin{array}{r}2148\\+4181\\\hline\end{array}$$

Worksheet 30, Hours and Half Hours

Name: _____ Date: _____

Draw the hour and minute hands.

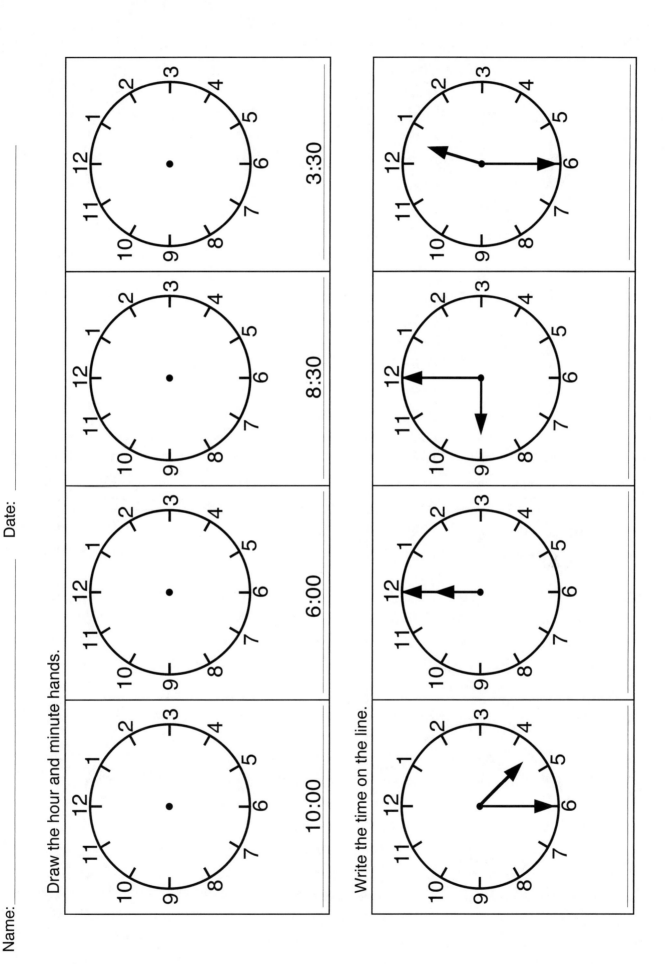

10:00   6:00   8:30   3:30

Write the time on the line.

Worksheet 31, Hours and Minutes

Name: _____ Date: _____

Draw the hour and minute hands.

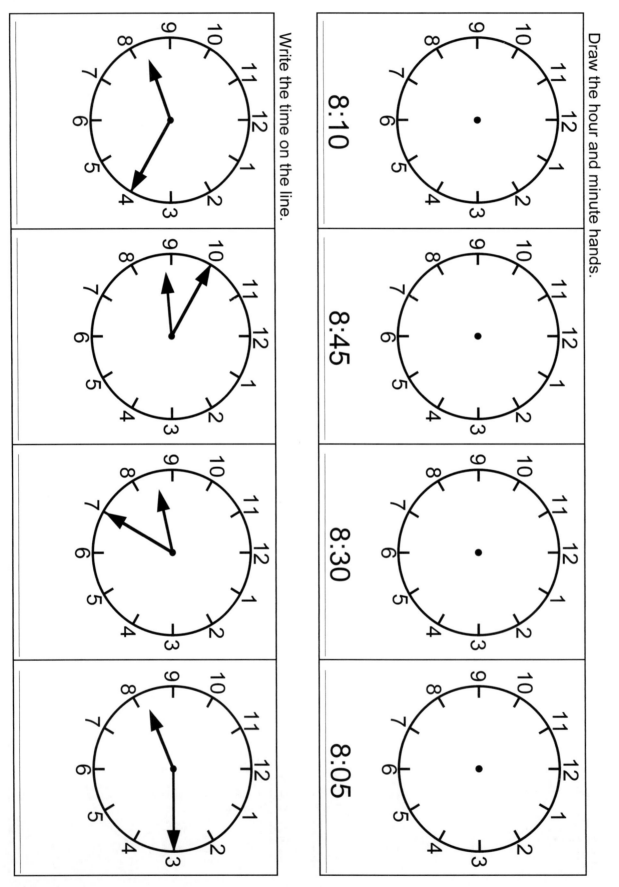

Write the time on the line.

Worksheet 32, Adding 4-Digit Numbers on Paper

Name: _____

Date: _____

```
   4 8 2 9              2 4 6 7
 + 3 2 5 6            + 2 1 6 5
```

```
   7 2 1 5              4 7 6 5
 + 1 8 3 5            + 4 7 7 6
```

```
   2 3 5 8              8 7 9 4
 + 5 9 8 8            + 3 6 9 5
```

RightStart™ Mathematics second edition, B

© Activities for Learning, Inc. 2013, 2024

Worksheet 33-1, Adding Very Large Numbers

Name: _____

Date: _____

		9
	+	9

	+	9

	+	9

	+	9

	+	9

	+	9

	+	9

	+	9

	+	9

	1	2	3	4	5	6	7	9
+	1	2	3	4	5	6	7	9

+	1	2	3	4	5	6	7	9

+	1	2	3	4	5	6	7	9

+	1	2	3	4	5	6	7	9

+	1	2	3	4	5	6	7	9

+	1	2	3	4	5	6	7	9

+	1	2	3	4	5	6	7	9

+	1	2	3	4	5	6	7	9

+	1	2	3	4	5	6	7	9

RightStart™ Mathematics second edition, B

© Activities for Learning, Inc. 2013, 2024

Worksheet 33-2, Adding Very Large Numbers

Name: _____

Date: _____

	2	5
+	2	5

	2	5
+	2	5

	2	5
+	2	5

	2	5
+	2	5

	2	5
+	2	5

	2	5
+	2	5

	2	5
+	2	5

	2	5
+	2	5

	9	8	7	6	5	4	3	2
+	9	8	7	6	5	4	3	2

	9	8	7	6	5	4	3	2
+	9	8	7	6	5	4	3	2

	9	8	7	6	5	4	3	2
+	9	8	7	6	5	4	3	2

	9	8	7	6	5	4	3	2
+	9	8	7	6	5	4	3	2

	9	8	7	6	5	4	3	2
+	9	8	7	6	5	4	3	2

	9	8	7	6	5	4	3	2
+	9	8	7	6	5	4	3	2

	9	8	7	6	5	4	3	2
+	9	8	7	6	5	4	3	2

	9	8	7	6	5	4	3	2
+	9	8	7	6	5	4	3	2

RightStart™ Mathematics second edition, B

© Activities for Learning, Inc. 2013, 2024

Worksheet 34, Solving "Take From" Problems

Name:_____

Date: _____

Jay had 8 cherries and ate 3 of them. How many cherries does Jay have left?

_____

_____

Kate's book has 16 pages. She read 10 pages. How many pages does she have left to read?

_____

_____

The Day family is traveling 20 miles to a camp. They have driven 15 miles. How many more miles do they need to drive?

_____

_____

Alex had 12 eggs, which is a dozen. Alex dropped 3 eggs and they broke. How many eggs are not broken?

_____

_____

RightStart™ Mathematics second edition, B   © Activities for Learning, Inc. 2013, 2024

Worksheet 35, Subtraction as the Missing Addend

Name: _____   Date: _____

Find the missing addend by adding on in your head.

8 + ☐ = 10	5 + ☐ = 8	80 + ☐ = 90
28 + ☐ = 30	35 + ☐ = 40	20 + ☐ = 27
69 + ☐ = 73	7 + ☐ = 11	9 + ☐ = 15

Subtract by adding on in your head.

10 − 6 = ___	10 − 5 = ___	13 − 8 = ___
9 − 8 = ___	12 − 9 = ___	29 − 5 = ___
11 − 9 = ___	22 − 20 = ___	48 − 45 = ___
80 − 79 = ___	34 − 30 = ___	91 − 85 = ___
16 − 13 = ___	60 − 57 = ___	36 − 26 = ___

Worksheet 36, Subtracting Consecutive Numbers

Name: _____

Date: _____

Use strategies and do these in your head.

17 - 16 =	_____
84 - 82 =	_____
35 - 33 =	_____
41 - 39 =	_____
73 - 72 =	_____
60 - 58 =	_____
36 - 35 =	_____
31 - 30 =	_____
88 - 86 =	_____
18 - 17 =	_____

Worksheet 37, Subtracting by Taking Part from Ten

Name: _____

Date: _____

13 − 4 =	_____
15 − 7 =	_____
13 − 6 =	_____
14 − 6 =	_____
16 − 7 =	_____
12 − 3 =	_____
13 − 7 =	_____
16 − 9 =	_____
12 − 4 =	_____
14 − 8 =	_____

13 − 5 =	_____
12 − 7 =	_____
15 − 6 =	_____
13 − 8 =	_____
12 − 5 =	_____
14 − 5 =	_____
15 − 8 =	_____
12 − 6 =	_____
14 − 7 =	_____

RightStart™ Mathematics second edition, B · © Activities for Learning, Inc. 2013, 2024

Worksheet 38, Solving Compare Problems

Name: _____

Date: _____

Jamie walked 9 blocks. Kim walked 3 blocks farther. How far did Kim walk?

_____

_____

The difference between two numbers is 7. The larger number is 13. What is the smaller number?

_____

_____

In a certain year, February had 3 fewer days than January. January has 31 days. How many days did February have?

_____

_____

West Park has 8 trees. North Park has 14 trees. How many fewer trees does West Park have than North Park?

_____

_____

RightStart™ Mathematics second edition, B

© Activities for Learning, Inc. 2013, 2024

Worksheet 39, Addition and Subtraction Equations

Name: _____

Date: _____

Write = if the numbers are an equation. Write ≠ if they are not an equation.

3 + 2 __ 1 + 4
5 + 2 + 2 __ 10
14 __ 10 − 4
16 − 2 __ 14 + 2
102 __ 102

Use +, −, and = to make equations.

4 __ 3 __ 7
2 __ 10 __ 8
3 __ 3 __ 7 __ 1
16 __ 10 __ 3 __ 3
8 __ 0 __ 9 __ 1

RightStart™ Mathematics second edition, B   © Activities for Learning, Inc. 2013, 2024

Worksheet 40, Continuing Patterns in the Hundreds

Name: _____

Date: _____

350	360	370	_____	_____
690	700	710	_____	_____
200	205	210	_____	_____
896	897	898	_____	_____
480	490	500	_____	_____

797	798	799	_____	_____
198	199	200	_____	_____
425	430	435	_____	_____
890	895	900	_____	_____
870	880	890	_____	_____

490	495	500	_____	_____
502	501	500	_____	_____
200	300	400	_____	_____
302	402	502	_____	_____
200	225	250	_____	_____

RightStart™ Mathematics second edition, B

© Activities for Learning, Inc. 2013, 2024

Worksheet 41, Higher Even and Odd Numbers

Name: _____

Date: _____

Color all the even numbers.

1	2	3	4	5	6	7	8	9	10
11	12	13	14	15	16	17	18	19	20
21	22	23	24	25	26	27	28	29	30
31	32	33	34	35	36	37	38	39	40
41	42	43	44	45	46	47	48	49	50
51	52	53	54	55	56	57	58	59	60
61	62	63	64	65	66	67	68	69	70
71	72	73	74	75	76	77	78	79	80
81	82	83	84	85	86	87	88	89	90
91	92	93	94	95	96	97	98	99	100

Color all the odd numbers.

1	2	3	4	5	6	7	8	9	10
11	12	13	14	15	16	17	18	19	20
21	22	23	24	25	26	27	28	29	30
31	32	33	34	35	36	37	38	39	40
41	42	43	44	45	46	47	48	49	50
51	52	53	54	55	56	57	58	59	60
61	62	63	64	65	66	67	68	69	70
71	72	73	74	75	76	77	78	79	80
81	82	83	84	85	86	87	88	89	90
91	92	93	94	95	96	97	98	99	100

RightStart™ Mathematics second edition, B

© Activities for Learning, Inc. 2013, 2024

Worksheet 42, Greater Than or Less Than Symbols

Name: _____ Date: _____

Write <, >, or = in the ◯.

104 ◯ 140	9 + 4 ◯ 10 + 4
76 ◯ 67	24 + 85 ◯ 85 + 24
213 ◯ 231	25 + 10 ◯ 30 + 5
1024 ◯ 124	100 + 7 ◯ 106
6009 ◯ 609	7 + 7 ◯ 8 + 6
550 ◯ 5500	19 + 16 ◯ 15 + 15
517 ◯ 715	14 + 14 ◯ 50

Worksheet 43, Introducing Area

Name: _____

Date: _____

Write = or ≠ in the circles to show if the areas in a row are equal or are not equal.

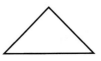

 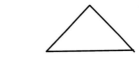

  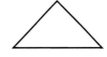

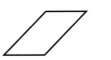

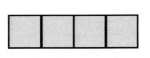

Worksheet 44, Halves and Fourths

Cut apart the five rectangles.

Worksheet 45, Fourths and Quarters

Cut out the circle.

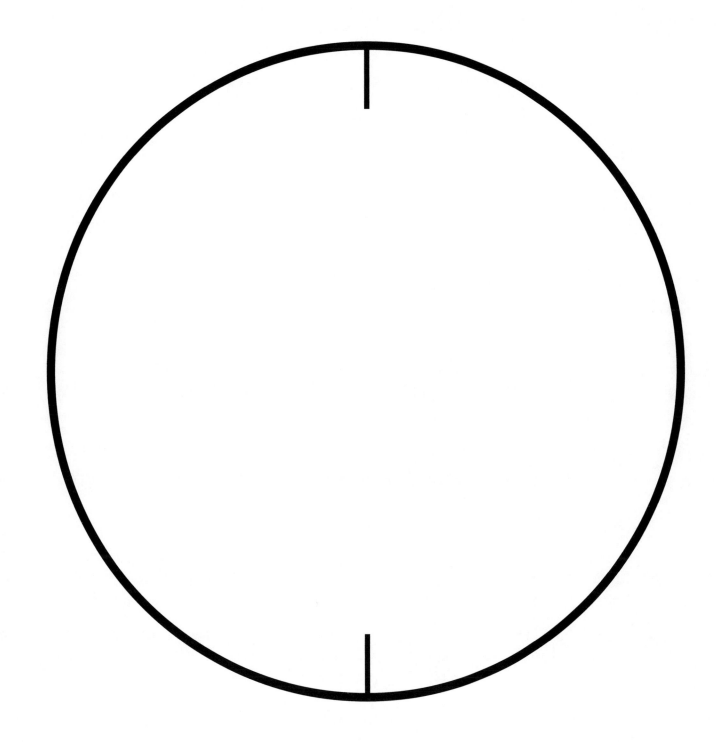

Worksheet 46, Measuring with Centimeters

Name: _____ Date: _____

1. Measure the side of each tangram piece in centimeters and write it along the edge.

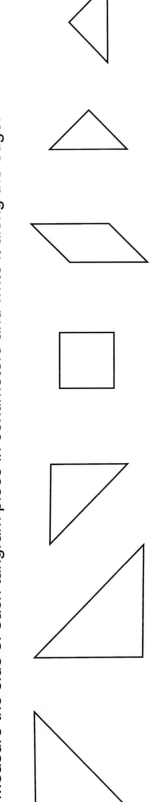

2. Write the total number of sides with each measurement.

10 cm	7 cm	5 cm	$3\frac{1}{2}$ cm

3. Write about your findings.

_____
_____
_____
_____

Worksheet 47-1, Graphing

Name: _____

Date: _____

1. Write the name of each person in the correct box.

People having 0 pockets.	People having 1 pocket.
People having 2 pockets.	People having 3 pockets.
People having 4 pockets.	People having >4 pockets.

2. Write the total number of people for each number of pockets.

0 pockets	1 pocket	2 pockets	3 pockets	4 pockets	>4 pockets

3. Fill in the graph.

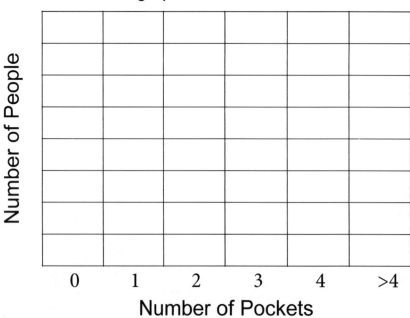

4. What number of pockets is most common? _____

Worksheet 47-2, Graphing

Name: _____

Date: _____

1. Write the name of each person in the correct box.

Name having 2 letters.	Name having 3 letters.
Name having 4 letters.	Name having 5 letters.
Name having 6 letters.	Name having >6 letters.

2. Write the total number of people for each number of letters.

2 letters	3 letters	4 letters	5 letters	6 letters	>6 letters

3. Fill in the graph.

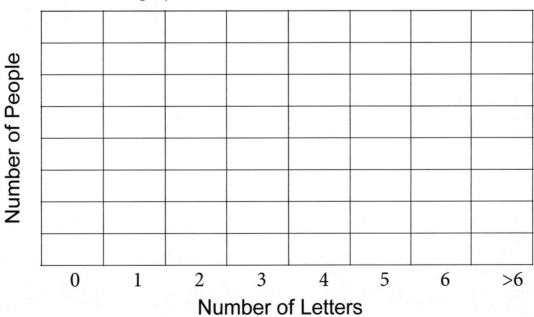

4. What number of letters is most common? _____

Worksheet 48, Measuring with Inches

Name: _____

Date: _____

Measure and write either cm or in.

2 ___

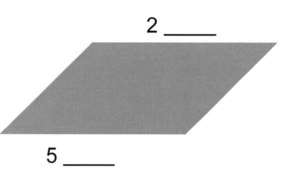

2 ___

5 ___

3 ½ ___

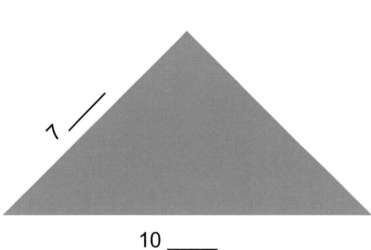

7 ___

10 ___

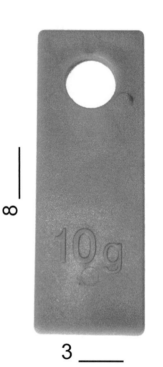

8 ___

3 ___

10 ___

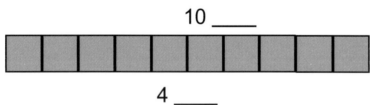

4 ___

15 ___

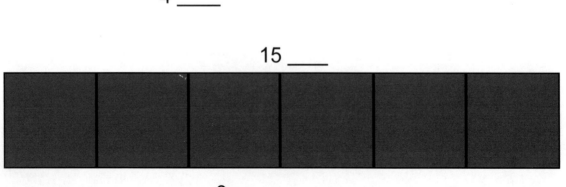

6 ___

Worksheet 49, Making Rectangles with Tiles

Name: _____

Date: _____

Use 8 tiles to make rectangles.

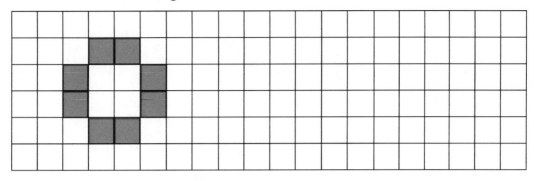

Use 16 tiles to make 4 rectangles. Find the number of tiles that could fit inside.

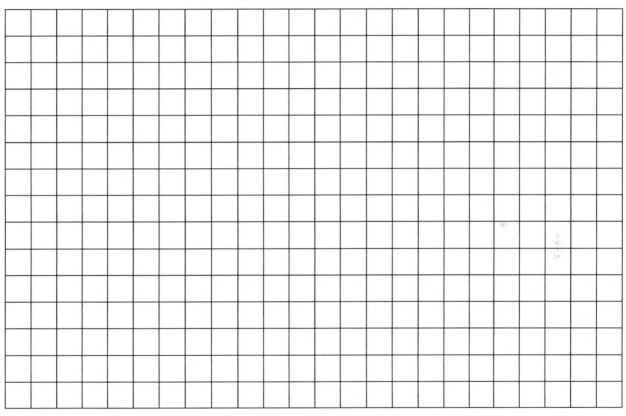

Use your ruler to measure three things in the room. Write what it is and how much it measures.

_____

_____

_____

Worksheet 50, Mentally Adding with Sums over 100

Name: _____   Date: _____

To see the pattern, find your answers and mark the squares.

101	102	103	104	105	106	107	108	109	110
111	112	113	114	115	116	117	118	119	120
121	122	123	124	125	126	127	128	129	130
131	132	133	134	135	136	137	138	139	140
141	142	143	144	145	146	147	148	149	150
151	152	153	154	155	156	157	158	159	160
161	162	163	164	165	166	167	168	169	170
171	172	173	174	175	176	177	178	179	180
181	182	183	184	185	186	187	188	189	190
191	192	193	194	195	196	197	198	199	200

42 + 80 = _____

76 + 80 = _____

52 + 60 = _____

94 + 50 = _____

44 + 90 = _____

85 + 50 = _____

88 + 90 = _____

99 + 90 = _____

98 + 90 = _____

87 + 80 = _____

75 + 70 = _____

96 + 70 = _____

99 + 80 = _____

67 + 90 = _____

73 + 50 = _____

83 + 30 = _____

Worksheet 51, Building with Cubes

Name: _____

Date: _____

How many cubes are in each set?

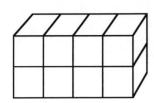 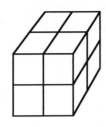 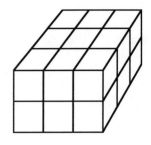

a. _____   b. _____   c. _____

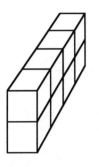 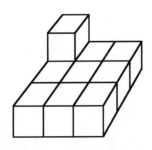 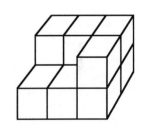

d. _____   e. _____   f. _____

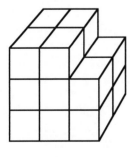 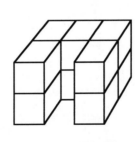 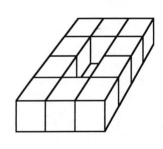

g. _____   h. _____   i. _____

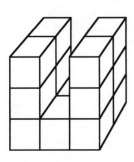 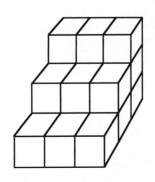 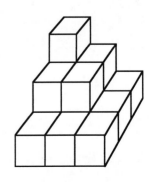

j. _____   k. _____   l. _____

Worksheet 52, Pennies, Nickels, and Dimes

Name: _____

Date: _____

Write the total value of the coins.

Worksheet 53, Choosing Coins

Name: _____ Date: _____

Circle the coins needed to make the amount.

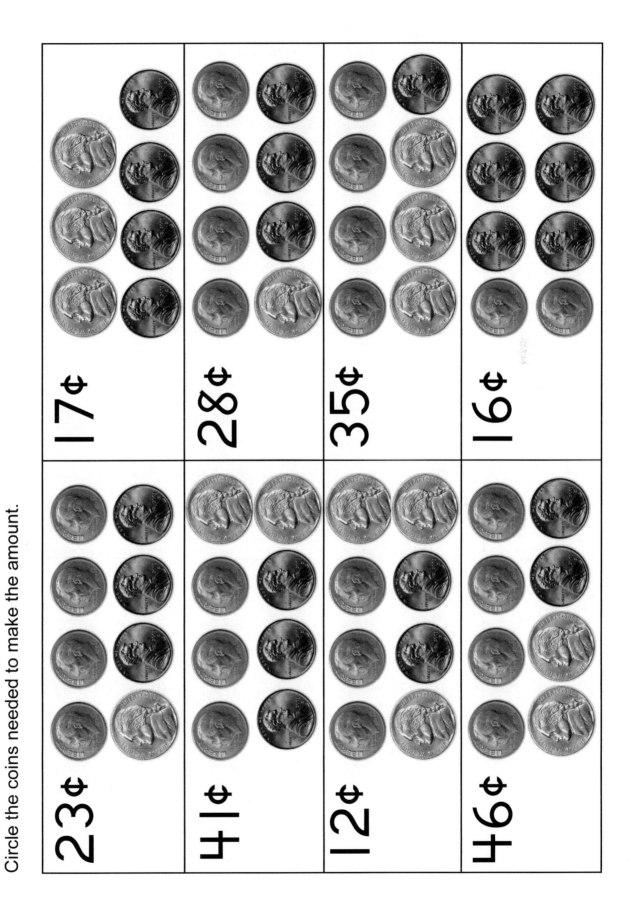

RightStart™ Mathematics second edition, B

Worksheet 54, Counting Money with Quarters

Name: _____ Date: _____

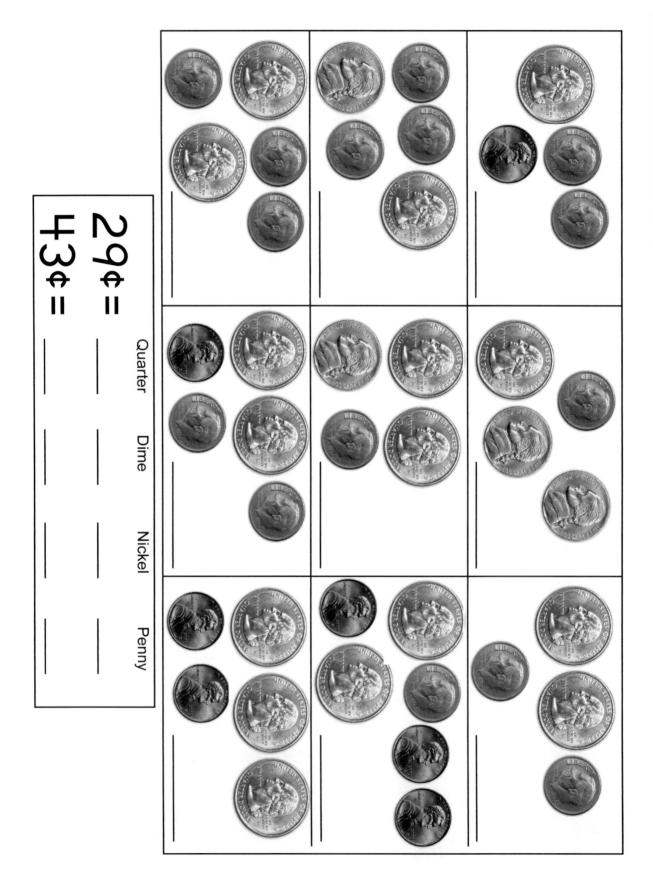

29¢ = ___ ___ ___ ___
43¢ = ___ ___ ___ ___
         Quarter Dime Nickel Penny

Worksheet 55, Introducing Multiplication as Arrays

Name: _____

Date: _____

5 × 2 = ___	5 × 5 = ___
8 × 2 = ___	7 × 3 = ___
10 × 5 = ___	2 × 6 = ___
4 × 2 = ___	4 × 5 = ___
6 × 4 = ___	2 × 2 = ___
3 × 3 = ___	6 × 5 = ___
4 × 3 = ___	9 × 4 = ___
6 × 10 = ___	9 × 6 = ___

Write the equations.

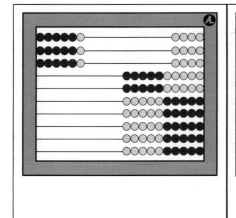 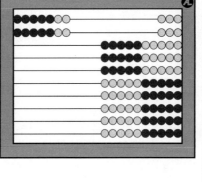 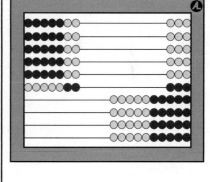

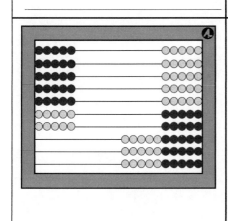 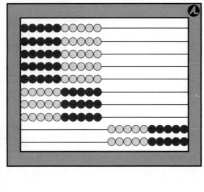 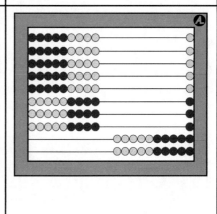

MATH JOURNAL

MATH JOURNAL

RightStart™ Mathematics second edition, B

© Activities for Learning, Inc. 2013, 2024

MATH JOURNAL

RightStart™ Mathematics second edition, B

© Activities for Learning, Inc. 2013, 2024

MATH JOURNAL

RightStart™ Mathematics second edition, B

© Activities for Learning, Inc. 2013, 2024

MATH JOURNAL

RightStart™ Mathematics second edition, B

© Activities for Learning, Inc. 2013, 2024

MATH JOURNAL

RightStart™ Mathematics second edition, B

© Activities for Learning, Inc. 2013, 2024

MATH JOURNAL

RightStart™ Mathematics second edition, B

© Activities for Learning, Inc. 2013, 2024

MATH JOURNAL

RightStart™ Mathematics second edition, B

© Activities for Learning, Inc. 2013, 2024

MATH JOURNAL

RightStart™ Mathematics second edition, B

© Activities for Learning, Inc. 2013, 2024

MATH JOURNAL

RightStart™ Mathematics second edition, B

© Activities for Learning, Inc. 2013, 2024

MATH JOURNAL

RightStart™ Mathematics second edition, B

© Activities for Learning, Inc. 2013, 2024

MATH JOURNAL

RightStart™ Mathematics second edition, B

© Activities for Learning, Inc. 2013, 2024

MATH JOURNAL

RightStart™ Mathematics second edition, B

© Activities for Learning, Inc. 2013, 2024

MATH JOURNAL

RightStart™ Mathematics second edition, B

© Activities for Learning, Inc. 2013, 2024

MATH JOURNAL

RightStart™ Mathematics second edition, B

© Activities for Learning, Inc. 2013, 2024

MATH JOURNAL

RightStart™ Mathematics second edition, B

© Activities for Learning, Inc. 2013, 2024

MATH JOURNAL

RightStart™ Mathematics second edition, B

© Activities for Learning, Inc. 2013, 2024

MATH JOURNAL

MATH JOURNAL

RightStart™ Mathematics second edition, B

© Activities for Learning, Inc. 2013, 2024

MATH JOURNAL

RightStart™ Mathematics second edition, B

© Activities for Learning, Inc. 2013, 2024

MATH JOURNAL

RightStart™ Mathematics second edition, B

© Activities for Learning, Inc. 2013, 2024

MATH JOURNAL

RightStart™ Mathematics second edition, B

© Activities for Learning, Inc. 2013, 2024

Sums Practice 1

Name: _____

Date: _____

$$\begin{array}{r} 9599 \\ +106 \\ \hline \end{array}$$

$$\begin{array}{r} 2563 \\ +3861 \\ \hline \end{array}$$

$$\begin{array}{r} 7932 \\ +1452 \\ \hline \end{array}$$

$$\begin{array}{r} 2787 \\ +5633 \\ \hline \end{array}$$

$$\begin{array}{r} 1655 \\ +7181 \\ \hline \end{array}$$

$$\begin{array}{r} 7667 \\ +432 \\ \hline \end{array}$$

$$\begin{array}{r} 3378 \\ +7865 \\ \hline \end{array}$$

$$\begin{array}{r} 3568 \\ +4636 \\ \hline \end{array}$$

RightStart™ Mathematics second edition, B

© Activities for Learning, Inc. 2013, 2024

Sums Practice 2

Name: _____

Date: _____

$$\begin{array}{r} 2841 \\ +\ 7159 \\ \hline \end{array}$$

$$\begin{array}{r} 1533 \\ +\ 1336 \\ \hline \end{array}$$

$$\begin{array}{r} 3293 \\ +\ 6513 \\ \hline \end{array}$$

$$\begin{array}{r} 6944 \\ +\ 6482 \\ \hline \end{array}$$

$$\begin{array}{r} 3625 \\ +\ 8375 \\ \hline \end{array}$$

$$\begin{array}{r} 6856 \\ +\ 984 \\ \hline \end{array}$$

$$\begin{array}{r} 2999 \\ +\ 2468 \\ \hline \end{array}$$

$$\begin{array}{r} 3751 \\ +\ 9356 \\ \hline \end{array}$$

RightStart™ Mathematics second edition, B   © Activities for Learning, Inc. 2013, 2024

Sums Practice 3

Name: _____

Date: _____

$$
\begin{array}{r}
7284 \\
+\ 1794 \\
\hline
\end{array}
$$

$$
\begin{array}{r}
9999 \\
+\quad\ \ 1 \\
\hline
\end{array}
$$

$$
\begin{array}{r}
4675 \\
+\ 5948 \\
\hline
\end{array}
$$

$$
\begin{array}{r}
7329 \\
+\ 6438 \\
\hline
\end{array}
$$

$$
\begin{array}{r}
8662 \\
+\quad 359 \\
\hline
\end{array}
$$

$$
\begin{array}{r}
9267 \\
+\ 6184 \\
\hline
\end{array}
$$

$$
\begin{array}{r}
7298 \\
+\ 1953 \\
\hline
\end{array}
$$

$$
\begin{array}{r}
9337 \\
+\ 2273 \\
\hline
\end{array}
$$

Sums Practice 4

Name: _____

Date: _____

$$
\begin{array}{r}
1\ 3\ 5\ 7 \\
+\ 2\ 4\ 6\ 8 \\
\hline
\end{array}
$$

$$
\begin{array}{r}
2\ 1\ 3\ 7 \\
+\ 6\ 1\ 6\ 4 \\
\hline
\end{array}
$$

$$
\begin{array}{r}
1\ 3\ 9\ 8 \\
+\ 1\ 4\ 0\ 6 \\
\hline
\end{array}
$$

$$
\begin{array}{r}
3\ 1\ 4\ 9 \\
+\ 7\ 7\ 8\ 8 \\
\hline
\end{array}
$$

$$
\begin{array}{r}
9\ 3\ 8\ 5 \\
+\ \ \ \ \ 9\ 9 \\
\hline
\end{array}
$$

$$
\begin{array}{r}
2\ 9\ 2\ 5 \\
+\ 1\ 4\ 6\ 4 \\
\hline
\end{array}
$$

$$
\begin{array}{r}
2\ 9\ 7\ 6 \\
+\ 2\ 9\ 7\ 6 \\
\hline
\end{array}
$$

$$
\begin{array}{r}
3\ 7\ 5\ 1 \\
+\ 4\ 2\ 1\ 6 \\
\hline
\end{array}
$$

RightStart™ Mathematics second edition, B

© Activities for Learning, Inc. 2013, 2024

Sums Practice 5

Name: _____

Date: _____

$$
\begin{array}{r}
3286 \\
+\ 9041 \\
\hline
\end{array}
$$

$$
\begin{array}{r}
5599 \\
+\ 1217 \\
\hline
\end{array}
$$

$$
\begin{array}{r}
6474 \\
+\ 1593 \\
\hline
\end{array}
$$

$$
\begin{array}{r}
4637 \\
+\ 6513 \\
\hline
\end{array}
$$

$$
\begin{array}{r}
2358 \\
+\ 3397 \\
\hline
\end{array}
$$

$$
\begin{array}{r}
1997 \\
+\ 2786 \\
\hline
\end{array}
$$

$$
\begin{array}{r}
5075 \\
+\ 3873 \\
\hline
\end{array}
$$

$$
\begin{array}{r}
8342 \\
+\ 6394 \\
\hline
\end{array}
$$

Sums Practice 6

Name: _____

Date: _____

Write these numbers in the columns and add.

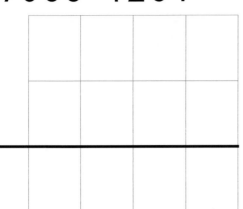
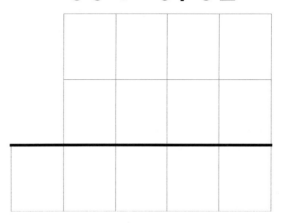
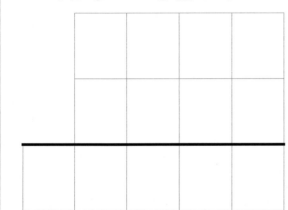
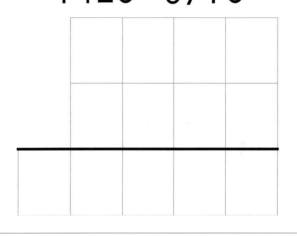
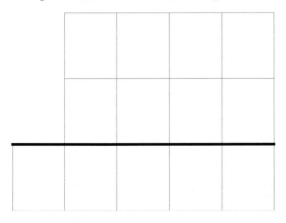
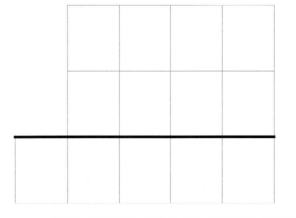

Sums Practice 7

Name: _____

Date: _____

Write these numbers in the columns and add.

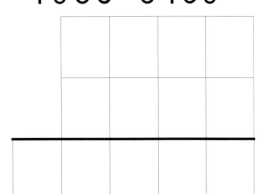

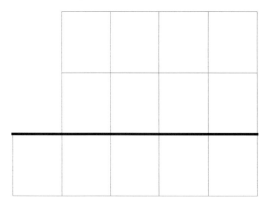

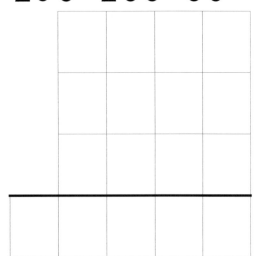

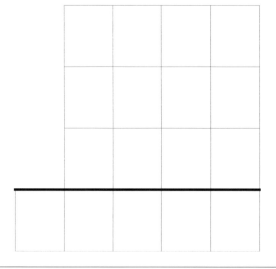

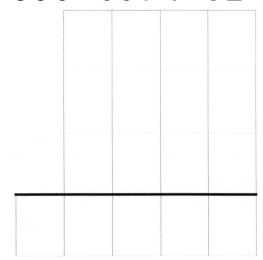

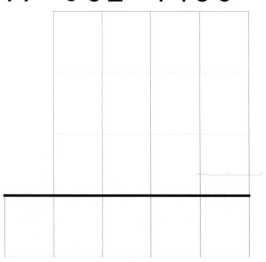

Sums Practice 8

Name: ___
Date: ___

=	=	=	=	=	=	=	=	=	=
2	6	4	0	1	5	3	8	9	7
+	+	+	+	+	+	+	+	+	+
—	—	—	—	—	—	—	—	—	—

=	=	=	=	=	=	=	=	=	=
—	—	—	—	—	—	—	—	—	—
+	+	+	+	+	+	+	+	+	+
6	2	0	1	9	5	4	7	3	8

RightStart™ Mathematics second edition, B

Sums Practice 9

Name: _____   Date: _____

$6 + 2 =$

$0 + 2 =$

$2 + 2 =$

$1 + 2 =$

$7 + 2 =$

$3 + 2 =$

$4 + 2 =$

$8 + 2 =$

$7 + 2 =$

$5 + 2 =$

$2 + 4 =$

$2 + 1 =$

$2 + 8 =$

$2 + 5 =$

$2 + 7 =$

$2 + 6 =$

$2 + 2 =$

$2 + 7 =$

$2 + 0 =$

$2 + 3 =$

RightStart™ Mathematics second edition, B   © Activities for Learning, Inc. 2013, 2024

Sums Practice 10

Name: _____

Date: _____

$6 + \underline{} = 10$

$9 + \underline{} = 10$

$3 + \underline{} = 10$

$1 + \underline{} = 10$

$7 + \underline{} = 10$

$2 + \underline{} = 10$

$4 + \underline{} = 10$

$8 + \underline{} = 10$

$5 + \underline{} = 10$

$10 + \underline{} = 10$

$5 + 2 = \underline{}$

$5 + 0 = \underline{}$

$1 + 5 = \underline{}$

$5 + 3 = \underline{}$

$2 + 5 = \underline{}$

$4 + 5 = \underline{}$

$5 + 1 = \underline{}$

$3 + 5 = \underline{}$

$5 + 4 = \underline{}$

$5 + 5 = \underline{}$

RightStart™ Mathematics second edition, B

© Activities for Learning, Inc. 2013, 2024

Sums Practice 11

Name: _____ Date: _____

___ + 4 = 10	___ + 1 = 10	___ + 6 = 10	___ + 5 = 10	___ + 7 = 10	___ + 2 = 10	___ + 0 = 10	___ + 3 = 10	___ + 9 = 10	___ + 8 = 10

4 = 1 + ___	5 = 1 + ___	4 = 2 + ___	5 = 2 + ___	3 = 1 + ___	4 = 3 + ___	2 = 1 + ___	3 = 2 + ___	5 = 3 + ___	5 = 4 + ___

RightStart™ Mathematics second edition, B

Sums Practice 12

Name: _____ Date: _____

$3 + 5 =$	$1 + 2 =$	$2 + 6 =$	$9 + 1 =$	$2 + 5 =$
$8 + 2 =$	$2 + 3 =$	$6 + 3 =$	$1 + 7 =$	$4 + 4 =$

$2 + 2 =$	$7 + 1 =$	$3 + 6 =$	$5 + 4 =$	$8 + 1 =$
$4 + 2 =$	$1 + 9 =$	$4 + 5 =$	$3 + 2 =$	$7 + 3 =$

RightStart™ Mathematics second edition, B   © Activities for Learning, Inc. 2013, 2024

Sums Practice 13

Name: _____ Date: _____

5 + 5 =	6 + 1 =	5 + 3 =	1 + 3 =	6 + 4 =	4 + 3 =	1 + 8 =	6 + 2 =	3 + 7 =	1 + 6 =

7 + 2 =	3 + 3 =	5 + 2 =	2 + 8 =	1 + 4 =	2 + 4 =	4 + 6 =	1 + 5 =	2 + 7 =	3 + 4 =

RightStart™ Mathematics second edition, B   © Activities for Learning, Inc. 2013, 2024

ASSESSMENT

End of Year Assessment 1

Name: _____

Date: _____

1. Write the numbers 108 through 118 in the blanks below.

____ ____ ____ ____ ____ ____ ____ ____ ____ ____ ____

2–4. Find and circle the numbers that are said.

9087	980	978	987
372	2037	2307	237
786	687	7086	7860

5–8. Write <, >, or = in the circles.

$7 + 8 \bigcirc 8 + 7$
$1 + 90 \bigcirc 19$
$200 \bigcirc 50 + 50$
$100 + 1 \bigcirc 110$

9–15. Add.

$56 + 6 =$ ____	$37 + 5 =$ ____
$57 + 7 =$ ____	$85 + 8 =$ ____
$47 + 8 =$ ____	$77 + 10 =$ ____
$88 + 9 =$ ____	

End of Year Assessment 1

16. Solve the following problem and write the equation.

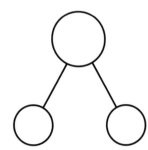

Twenty-two children will ride the train at the zoo. Eleven children are already on the train. How many more children must still get on the train?

_____

17–22. Subtract.

80 − 79 = ___	16 − 13 = ___
34 − 30 = ___	60 − 57 = ___
91 − 85 = ___	36 − 26 = ___

23–26. Add.

```
  1 3 9 8          3 1 4 9
+ 1 4 0 6        + 7 7 8 8
---------        ---------
```

```
  9 3 8 5          2 9 2 5
+     9 9        + 1 4 6 4
---------        ---------
```

End of Year Assessment 2

Name:_____

Date: _____

Circle the answer to the question said.

1. Sum   Difference   Equation

2. Sum   Difference   Equation

3–4. Solve the following problems.

Matt has a book with 43 pages and Emily has a book with 61 pages. Whose book has more pages and how many more?

_____

Kevin walked 23 blocks. Penny walked 8 blocks farther. How far did Penny walk?

_____

5–9. Complete the following equations.

| 4 _ 3 _ 7 |
| 2 _ 10 _ 8 |
| 3 _ 3 _ 7 _ 1 |
| 16 _ 10 _ 3 _ 3 |
| 8 _ 0 _ 9 _ 1 |

10–17. Write whether the following numbers are even or odd.

36 _____   83 _____   14 _____   22 _____

57 _____   99 _____   40 _____   19 _____

End of Year Assessment 3

Name: _____

Date: _____

1–7. Measure the sides of the tangram pieces with the centimeter cubes and write the results along the sides of the matching pieces below.

8–9. Solve the following problems.

Jason measured a side of the Cotter Abacus and found it was 19. What were Jason's units, centimeters or inches?

_____

Jessica measured the length of 10 abacus beads. She found it was 4. What were Jessica's units, centimeters or inches?

_____

10. How many centimeters is 4 inches? _____

11. How many centimeters is 2 inches? _____

RightStart™ Mathematics second edition, B   © Activities for Learning, Inc. 2013, 2024

End of Year Assessment 3

12. Measure the longest side of the large tangram triangle and write your findings below.

13–19. Find and circle all the sides of the tangram pieces that measure 2 inches. Write the total found on the line below.

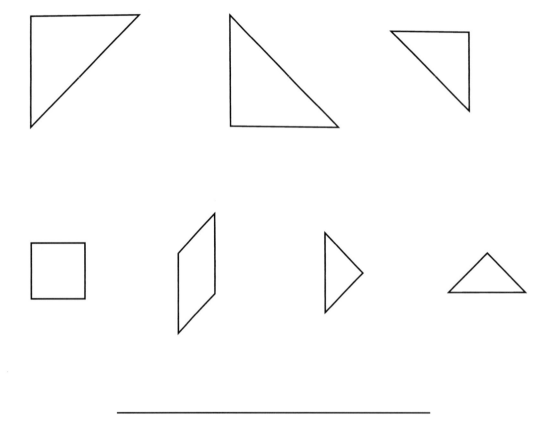

End of Year Assessment 4

Name: _____

Date: _____

Look at the tangram piece your teacher is pointing to and answer the following questions.

1. Is this a quadrilateral? _____

2. What is it called? _____

3. Does it have any parallel lines? _____

Look at the 7 tangram pieces shown and answer the following questions.

4. How many of the pieces are right triangles? _____

5. How many right angles are there in all the pieces? _____

6. How many pieces are rectangles? _____

7. How many triangles are there? _____

8. How many of the pieces are parallelograms? _____

9. How many of the pieces have parallel lines? _____

10. How many pieces have perpendicular lines? _____

Look at the geometry solids and answer the following questions.

11. How many solids are prisms? _____

12. How many solids are pyramids? _____

13. Do the prisms have parallel lines? _____

RightStart™ Mathematics second edition, B   © Activities for Learning, Inc. 2013, 2024

End of Year Assessment 4

14. Do the prisms have perpendicular lines? _____

15. What shape are the sides of the pyramid? _____

16. How many solids are cylinders? _____

17. Draw a line under the circle that is divided in half.

18. Draw a line under circle that is divided into fourths.

19. How many quarters are in a whole? _____

20. How many quarters in a half? _____

21. What is another word for quarter? _____

22. How many right angles do you see at the center of the circle? _____

RightStart™ Mathematics second edition, B   © Activities for Learning, Inc. 2013, 2024

Certificate of Achievement

Presented to

_____

for completing

RIGHTSTART™ MATHEMATICS
LEVEL B
Second Edition

On this _____ day of _____

_____ ,Teacher

Joan A. Cotter, Ph.D.

Tracy Mittleider, MSEd